Natural Laboratories:
Scientists in
National Parks

GATES OF THE
ARCTIC

Ruth A. Musgrave

Rourke
Educational Media

rourkeeducationalmedia.com

Before, During, and After Reading Activities

Before Reading: Building Background Knowledge and Academic Vocabulary

"Before Reading" strategies activate prior knowledge and set a purpose for reading. Before reading a book, it is important to tap into what your child or students already know about the topic. This will help them develop their vocabulary and increase their reading comprehension.

Questions and activities to build background knowledge:
1. Look at the cover of the book. What will this book be about?
2. What do you already know about the topic?
3. Let's study the Table of Contents. What will you learn about in the book's chapters?
4. What would you like to learn about this topic? Do you think you might learn about it from this book? Why or why not?

Building Academic Vocabulary

Building academic vocabulary is critical to understanding subject content.
Assist your child or students to gain meaning of the following vocabulary words.
Content Area Vocabulary
Read the list. What do these words mean?

- adorn
- backcountry
- baseline
- ecosystem
- hardy
- indicators
- intact
- migrate
- nomadic
- prehistoric
- remote
- subarctic

During Reading: Writing Component

"During Reading" strategies help to make connections, monitor understanding, generate questions, and stay focused.
1. While reading, write in your reading journal any questions you have or anything you do not understand.
2. After completing each chapter, write a summary of the chapter in your reading journal.
3. While reading, make connections with the text and write them in your reading journal.
   a) Text to Self – What does this remind me of in my life? What were my feelings when I read this?
   b) Text to Text – What does this remind me of in another book I've read? How is this different from other books I've read?
   c) Text to World – What does this remind me of in the real world? Have I heard about this before? (News, current events, school, etc....)

After Reading: Comprehension and Extension Activity

"After Reading" strategies provide an opportunity to summarize, question, reflect, discuss, and respond to text. After reading the book, work on the following questions with your child or students to check their level of reading comprehension and content mastery.
1. What makes the Gates of the Arctic a challenging place to study? (Summarize)
2. Why is the Gates of the Arctic an important national park? (Infer)
3. What do scientists learn through archaeological digs? (Asking Questions)
4. What features of the park would you be most interested in studying as a park scientist? (Text to Self Connection)

Extension Activity
Pick a wild animal or plant that lives near you. If you were a scientist, how would you study it? What do you already know about it? What would you like to know? What kinds of questions would you need to answer in order to protect it? Is there anything you could invent to help study or protect it?

TABLE OF CONTENTS

THE ARCTIC CIRCLE

Wind, temperature, water, earthquakes, and time created the Gates of the Arctic's stunning landscape. Rivers, mountains, forests, and glaciers **adorn** this unspoiled land.

Black spruce trees grow in flat frozen ground in the Arctic Circle.

The vast lands of the Gates of the Arctic include glaciers, mountains, valleys, rivers, and streams.

Arctic Reach

The Arctic includes everything north of the Arctic Circle, which is approximately 66 degrees, 34 minutes north latitude.

The Gates of the Arctic National Park and Preserve is in Alaska within the Arctic Circle. The 8.5 million acre (3.44 million hectare) park is bigger than the state of Maryland.

The Gates of the Arctic habitat has remained virtually the same since the first **nomadic** hunters arrived 13 thousand years ago. There are no roads, businesses, trails, or campgrounds. Visitors bring everything they need to survive when they backpack, dog sled, or fly in on a bush plane.

Thousands of years ago the first hunters found a stunning landscape rich with wildlife.

Strange Days

Because of the tilt of the Earth, it is dark 24 hours a day in the winter and light 24 hours a day in the summer.

The sun still shines at midnight in the middle of the summer in the Arctic.

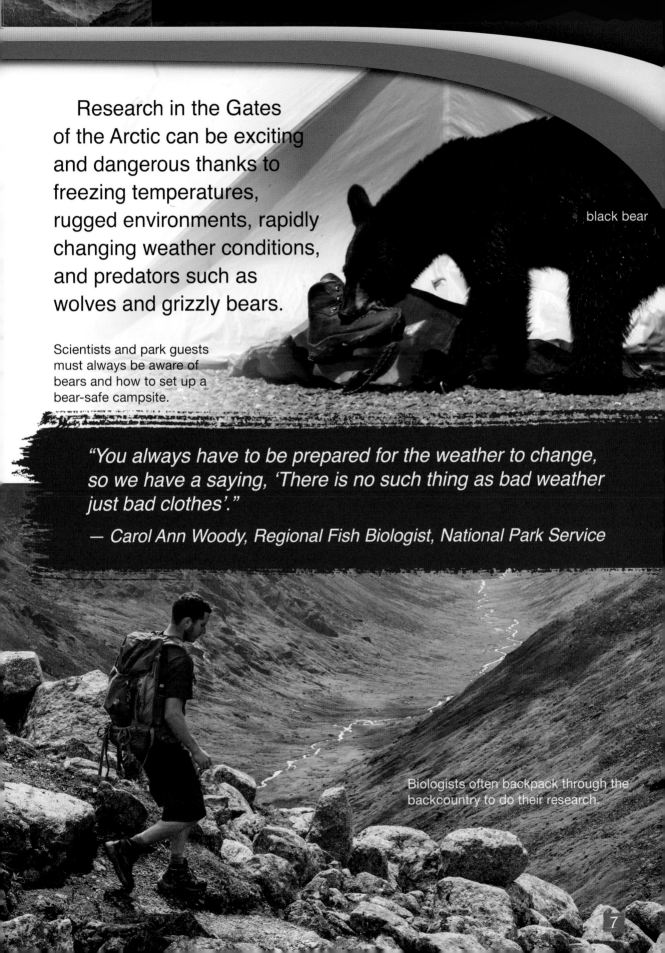

Research in the Gates of the Arctic can be exciting and dangerous thanks to freezing temperatures, rugged environments, rapidly changing weather conditions, and predators such as wolves and grizzly bears.

black bear

Scientists and park guests must always be aware of bears and how to set up a bear-safe campsite.

"You always have to be prepared for the weather to change, so we have a saying, 'There is no such thing as bad weather just bad clothes'."

— Carol Ann Woody, Regional Fish Biologist, National Park Service

Biologists often backpack through the backcountry to do their research.

CHAPTER TWO

WEATHER AND CLIMATE

Plants and animals must be **hardy** to survive in the Gates of the Arctic. The temperatures range between minus-20 to minus-50 degrees Fahrenheit (-29 to -46 degrees Celsius) most of the year.

A scientist uses special equipment to gather weather data.

Dr. Pam Sousanes is a physical scientist with the United States National Park Service. She studies weather and climate. The information she gathers helps scientists determine how warming temperatures or less snow will affect the wildlife, plants, and the rivers and lakes within the Gates of the Arctic.

Plants, like these ice and snow covered black spruce trees, must be hardy to survive the bitter cold.

Pam uses state-of-the-art weather stations to gather data. The weather stations are placed in some of the most **remote** locations. The stations constantly measure the temperature, humidity, wind speed, rainfall, snow depth, and soil temperatures. The information is sent to a satellite every hour. Scientists track the weather in real time from their computers.

Automated weather stations collect weather data throughout the park.

Wild Weather

The weather stations can withstand temperatures colder than minus-50 degrees Fahrenheit (-46 degrees Celsius) and 100 mile (161 kilometer) per hour winds.

Pam also analyzes the weather throughout the year from the data collected by the weather stations. Then she and other scientists discuss any patterns between the weather and behavior of animals, such as when the bears come out of their dens in the spring, if the caribou had enough to eat, or other observations.

CHAPTER THREE

THE LAND

Because of the extreme and constant freezing temperatures, the Gates of the Arctic is a permafrost **ecosystem**. That means, except for a thin layer that thaws in the summer, the ground remains frozen year-round. Permafrost is a vital part of the arctic and **subarctic** environments. Permafrost determines what kinds of plants and animals can survive in the Arctic.

This cross section of ground shows the frozen earth just beneath the thin thawed layer at the surface.

In some places in the Arctic, the ground has been frozen for thousands of years.

Permafrost is sensitive to climate change. Scientists are concerned the permafrost will thaw if there is long-term warming of the climate. This would cause catastrophic problems throughout the Arctic and to the animals, plants, and people. Scientists monitor permafrost by measuring the amount of ground that thaws in the summer.

Scientists use different methods to measure the depth of the permafrost.

Scientists use a long hollow tube to drill into the ground and remove a core sample of soil in order to measure the depth of thawing and permafrost.

Trees, shrubs, flowering plants, moss, and lichens grow in the Gates of the Arctic. The leaves, berries, roots, bark, and other plant parts are important food for caribou, muskox, bears, hares, birds, insects, and other animals.

Caribou search for food in the tundra and boreal forest.

Lichen, like this reindeer moss, grow slowly and live a very long time.

Arctic Plants

Due to the short Arctic summers, plants only have about 130 days to grow. As winter approaches, some plants die. Others stop growing. Some plants lose their leaves and others use the dead leaves to protect themselves from the ice and snow.

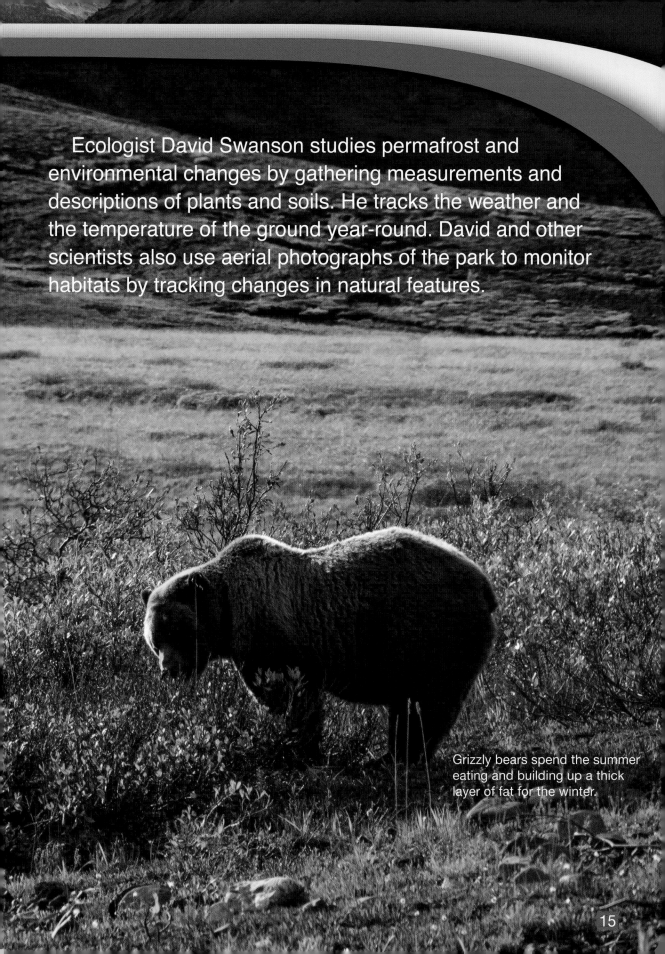

Ecologist David Swanson studies permafrost and environmental changes by gathering measurements and descriptions of plants and soils. He tracks the weather and the temperature of the ground year-round. David and other scientists also use aerial photographs of the park to monitor habitats by tracking changes in natural features.

Grizzly bears spend the summer eating and building up a thick layer of fat for the winter.

The boreal forest runs through the Gates of the Arctic. It thrives in freezing cold temperatures, short summers, and forest fires. The boreal forest wraps around the top of the world like a crown. It is the largest **intact** forest in the world and continues across northern North America, Siberia, northern Asia, and northern Europe.

The boreal forest (noted on this map in green) circles the top of the world.

Rivers run through the boreal forest.

The tundra connects to the boreal forest. Like the boreal forest, the tundra faces long winters and short summers. Unlike the boreal forest, though, the tundra is treeless. It rarely snows or rains in the tundra, making it a very cold desert.

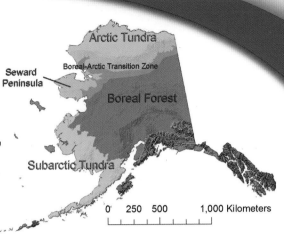

Arctic Tundra

Boreal-Arctic Transition Zone

Seward Peninsula

Boreal Forest

Subarctic Tundra

0   250   500   1,000 Kilometers

Many animals eat the leaves, nectar, and berries from the bearberry plant.

Short Summers, Short Plants

The constant cold, wind, and short summers make it hard for large plants to grow. Tundra plants are small and grow close to the ground.

Molly Tedesche takes a depth hoar snow sample.

Molly Tedesche is a snow hydrologist. She studies changes in the snowfields in the Gates of the Arctic. Snowfields are small patches of permanent ice that have accumulated over many years. Snowfields might be melting throughout the world.

Scientists use satellite photos to monitor landscape changes. They also compare satellite images taken over many years to look for long-term environmental changes.

Satellite Image

Satellite Image

1952

1979

0   100 m

0   100 m

2005

2013

0   100 m

0   100 m

Ken D. Tape is a research associate professor. He uses satellite imagery and time-lapse photography to document and study changes in the park's landscape over time. Ken compares the aspects of the entire ecosystem including permafrost, plants, animals, and people and how they all interact.

Rivers, lakes, and ponds are important habitats throughout the Gates of the Arctic. Aquatic ecologist Amy Larsen is fascinated by lakes. She collects water samples and makes observations about aquatic plants and insects.

A network of streams and rivers flow through the Gates of the Arctic.

Studies in the field are an essential part of Amy's research.

"Each lake is unique, just like people, and I want to understand how they differ, how they are changing and why."

— Amy Larsen

Scientists analyze water collected from lakes.

Amy travels to the lakes in a small airplane. She uses special computer equipment to measure the temperature, oxygen, and amount of salt in the water. She looks for patterns in the data to figure out if or how the various lakes are alike or not.

Small planes are important modes of transportation and research tools for park scientists.

CHAPTER FOUR

SCIENTISTS AND ANIMALS

Most of the animals found in the Gates of the Arctic need huge areas of continuous unspoiled land to find enough food, water, and shelter. Some are adapted to stay in the Arctic year-round. Other animals **migrate** to different locations to find food or warmer weather.

snowshoe hare

Tundra swans spend their summer in the arctic tundra raising chicks and then migrate to other locations during the winter.

More than 100 bird species live in or migrate through the Gates of the Arctic. Birds are an important part of the food web. Scientists track patterns in bird migration, diet, and habitat use. Changes in birds' behavior, number of chicks, where they travel, or how long the birds live can be **indicators** of the health of the ecosystem.

Common goldeneyes nest in the boreal forest.

caribou herd

Male and female caribou grow antlers.

Thousands of caribou thunder through the park. Caribou migrate in gigantic herds. They travel more than two thousand miles (3,219 kilometers) a year. Alaska's largest herd, called the western herd, has more than 200 thousand animals.

Throughout the year, the western herd roams in and out of the Gates of the Arctic park all the way to Canada. They migrate throughout a 157 thousand square mile (406,628 square kilometer) area. That's about the size of California. Caribou eat plants and lichens. Wolves, bears, and people hunt caribou.

Caribou herds travel throughout the Gates of the Arctic.

Caribou are a primary food source for many indigenous people of the Arctic.

Gray wolf

Wildlife biologist Dr. Kyle Joly studies caribou. One way he does this is by tracking the movement of the herds. Kyle and the science team temporarily capture some of the caribou as they swim across the Kobuk River during their fall migration. The scientists put GPS tracking collars on the caribou.

To place a tracking collar on a caribou, Kyle gently restrains the young animal as it swims across the river.

Caribou are excellent swimmers.

The collars collect data such as where the caribou travel. The collars send the information to a computer database so Kyle can track the caribou's movement.

A scientist tends to a sedated caribou.

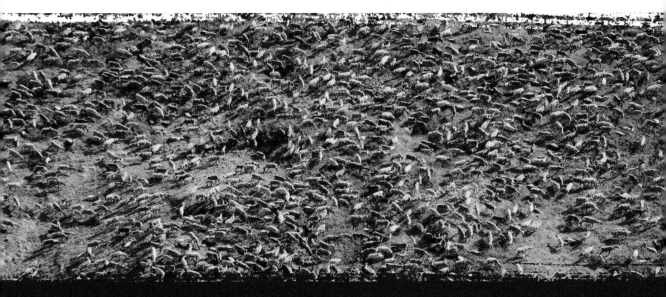

Tracking Population

Population studies are also an important part of caribou research. Scientists photograph herds from cameras mounted on small airplanes. The photos help scientists gather information on the

Kyle also studies brown bears. He wants to know what habitats they use to find food, where they make their dens, and the overall health of the population.

Some grizzly bears can eat as many as 30 salmon in a day.

Most of North America's brown bears live in Alaska. It is the second largest population worldwide.

Kyle uses GPS collars to track the bears. Scientists search for the bears from a helicopter. When they see one, they dart it with a tranquilizer and wait for it to fall asleep. A team then quickly measures the bear, collects genetic material, and places a GPS collar around its neck.

Scientists quickly measure a grizzly bear and attach a tracking collar before it wakes up.

Tracking collars use technology to send the bear's location and other information to a remote computer.

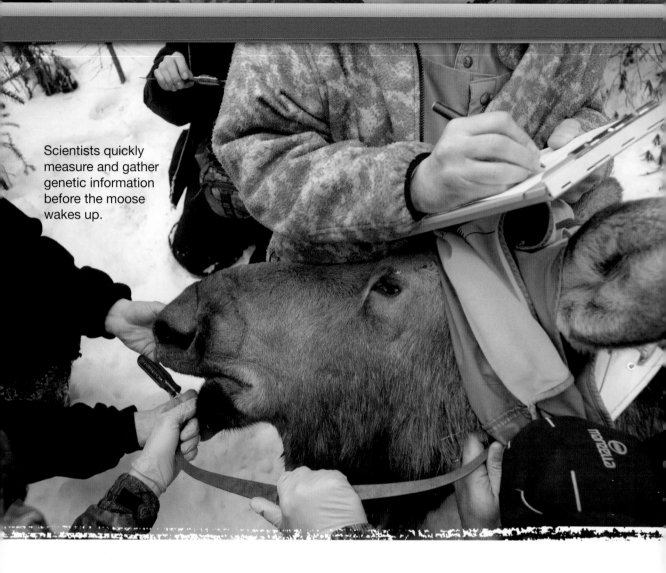

Scientists quickly measure and gather genetic information before the moose wakes up.

Moose are an important part of the boreal forest habitat. One of the ways Dr. Mathew Sorum studies moose populations is from the air. As scientists fly over an area in a small airplane, they count the number of moose or moose tracks they see and note the location.

Scientists believe the moose population might indicate long-term changes within the park's ecosystem. Fortunately, the most recent survey showed no changes in the moose population over the past ten years.

Moose calves grow quickly. They are born in the spring and independent from their mother by the fall.

Only the male moose grows antlers.

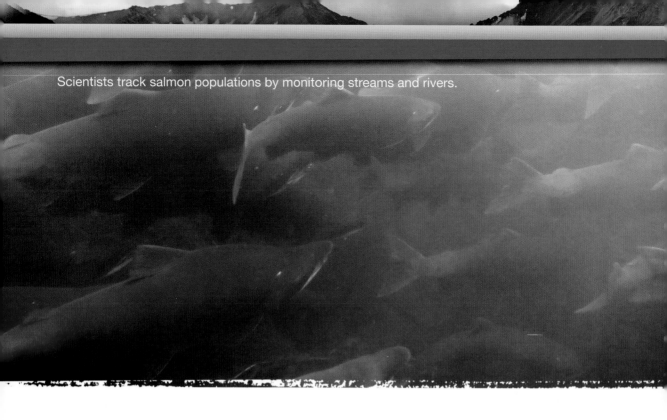
Scientists track salmon populations by monitoring streams and rivers.

Regional fish biologist Dr. Carol Ann Woody and a science crew take a helicopter from stream to stream to survey the park's fish. They measure, photograph, and collect data on each fish they catch then release them back into the stream.

Scientists quickly measure a salmon before returning it to the water.

People travel a long way to vacation and fish in the Gates of the Arctic.

Scientists map the fish locations and report them to the state of Alaska to ensure human activity and future plans do not affect their habitat. Salmon streams get special protections because they're an important food source for animals and indigenous people.

grizzly bear cubs hunting salmon

CHAPTER FIVE

THE PAST

Jeff Rasic, an archeologist for the Gates of the Arctic, studies the prehistory of ancient northern hunter-gatherers. Jeff and other archeologists work in remote, rugged, and often rarely explored areas of the park. They want to know how ancient people lived and how they used the land and resources.

Jeff measures and photographs artifacts before they are recovered from a site.

Park archaeologists estimate there are thousands of ancient sites to find and study.

Seeking the Past

To do their research, Jeff and the other archeologists travel into the wilderness on small planes, then hike or raft down rivers to look for sites.

Plane used for research

Scientists uncover an ancient artifact.

These carved bone tools were made by ancient people of Alaska.

Scientists uncover ancient campsites or hunting locations. They find tools made of stone, bones, and antlers. These artifacts tell scientists how the people hunted. Charcoal from ancient campfires and bones from **prehistoric** meals tell them what and where people ate thousands of years ago.

Archaeologists investigate a possible prehistoric site.

So far, Jeff and the other archeologists have discovered almost two thousand archaeological sites. Recently, they discovered a spearhead in the charcoal of an ancient campfire that dates back ten thousand years.

Paleoecologist Dr. Ben Gagliotti excavates and maps prehistoric plant and animal fossils. This helps scientists understand prehistoric wildlife and the human hunter-gatherers of the time.

Archaeologists search for clues on the purpose of some prehistoric artifacts, like these made from bone.

cm   AMR-186

Archaeologists find broken and complete spear and arrowheads created by ancient hunters.

Fossils found within the park date back 400 million years.

CHAPTER SIX

THE PRESENT

The Gates of the Arctic is home to Athapaskan, Nunamiut Eskimo, Eskimo people of the Kobuk and Noatak Rivers, and various non-native Alaskan people. Subsistence uses of Gates of the Arctic resources are a way of life and an essential part of their culture, tradition, and history. They rely on hunting, fishing, and plant gathering.

fish drying on a rack

"Subsistence is a way that native peoples of Alaska have preserved their cultures. This way of life is not confined to the land. It stretches out to the sky and the waters and rivers. The creatures of the Earth give themselves to the people, who in turn share with family and friends, shaping relationships that celebrate life."

— Helga Eakon, U.S. Fish and Wildlife Service Interagency Coordinator

Though some aspects of daily life might have changed, the plants, animals, and land continue to be essential to the Alaskan people.

Studies of long-term trends in the habitats and animal populations are key to understanding, managing, and protecting the animals and people that rely on the Gates of the Arctic ecosystem.

Caribou travel through the snowy grounds of the park.

Gates of the Arctic Wilderness is the third-largest designated wilderness area in the United States.

Within the park, designated wilderness areas have the highest level of protection. Wilderness Planner Kristin Pace makes sure the character of these areas is preserved.

Kristin works with the **backcountry** rangers to gather information and track conditions to determine the ideal **baseline** wilderness conditions. She also reviews human activities within the park to make sure they do not negatively affect the wilderness area.

"The Arctic requires a lot of preparation and flexibility. Nothing is certain when it comes to traveling in the Arctic. Surprises make life a lot more exciting."
— *Kristin Pace*

Scientists and visitors to the Gates of the Arctic must bring in everything they need to survive.

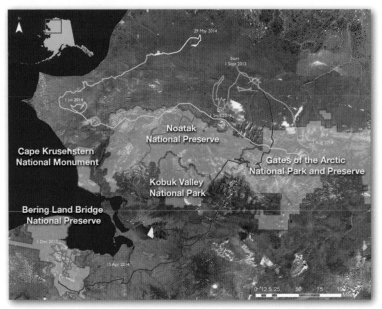

This map shows how caribou travel throughout Alaska.

The Gates of the Arctic is just one of the national parks in Alaska. Caribou and other animals migrate across Alaska and beyond. Scientists within the park work closely with researchers in connected parks through the Arctic Network Inventory and Monitoring Program. The Arctic Network includes five national parks and preserves in northern Alaska and represents some of the most remote and undisturbed places in the world.

A young caribou swims with the herd on its migration.

Caribou herds travel throughout Alaska and Canada.

The Arctic Network of Alaska Parklands encompasses miles of remote land.

Protecting Alaska's Wilderness

Parks in Alaska make up 60 percent of all the land within the U.S. National Park System. They include the most remote parks with more than 3,095 miles (4981 kilometers) of coastline and 52 million acres (21,043,653 hectares) of designated wilderness.

Alaska

National Parks

Scientists in the Gates of the Arctic monitor the health and populations of the plants, animals, and ecosystem in extreme conditions. This information is used to protect the habitats, animals, plants, food webs, and, in some cases, predict or track changes in climate.

Scientists in the park study the plants, animals, and even the frozen ground to help keep the entire ecosystem healthy.

"The purpose of Gates of the Arctic National Park and Preserve is to preserve the vast, wild, undeveloped character and environmental integrity of Alaska's central Brooks Range and to provide opportunities for wilderness recreation and traditional subsistence uses." —National Park Service

The Gates of the Arctic is a vast rugged natural laboratory just waiting for future scientists to explore.

DIGGING INTO THE PAST

Discover how scientists use clues from prehistoric campsites to learn about ancient people. Think like an archeologist and dig into your recycle bin!

Supplies

- clean items from the recycle bin
- paper
- pencil

Directions:

1. Carefully sort the items from a recycle bin with an adult's permission.

2. Figure out the best way to represent your data, such as graphs, writing, or art.

3. Think like a scientist and estimate how long ago the items were used and how many days it represents. What kinds of things can you learn about the people who used the items? What other information would be helpful to understand the people who used the items?

Glossary

adorn (uh-DORN): to decorate something

backcountry (BAK-kuhn-tree): a place that is remote and without roads or easy access

baseline (BASE-line): information or data used as the starting point or for comparison

ecosystem (EE-ko-sis-tuhm): an area including living things such as plants and animals and how they use or interact with nonliving things such as the landscape or weather

hardy (HAHR-dee): tough or strong

indicators (IN-di-kay-turz): information that points to or hints of some other information

intact (in-TAKT): not broken, in one piece, or not missing anything

migrate (MYE-grate): when animals travel from one place to another to find food, mates, or due to seasons

nomadic (noh-MAD-ik): a person or people who travel from place to place to find food or better weather rather than stay in one place or location

prehistoric (pree-hi-STOR-ik): relating to time before written language or history

remote (ri-MOHT): far from any city or towns, hard to get to or isolated

subarctic (suhb-AHR-tik): the area of the Earth just below the arctic or Arctic Circle

Index

Show What You Know

1. Who were the first people to utilize Gates of the Arctic lands and when did they arrive?

2. How do scientists use their research to protect resources and the environment?

3. What is the difference between a tundra and boreal forest?

4. How can monitoring caribou, moose, and other animals and their habitats help people around the world understand how they affect the ecosystem?

5. Why is the Gates of the Arctic important to Native Alaskan People?

Further Reading

Guiberson, Brenda Z., *Life in the Boreal Forest*, Square Fish, 2016.

National Parks Guide USA Centennial Edition: The Most Amazing Sights, Scenes, and Cool Activities from Coast to Coast! National Geographic Children's Books, 2016.

Woodford, Chris, *Arctic Tundra and Polar Deserts*, Raintree, 2003.

About the Author

Ruth A. Musgrave talks with turtles, has seastars in her eyes, and counts sharks among her most trusted friends. Ruth is also an award-winning author of hundreds of articles about animals and more than 19 books including *Mission Shark Rescue: All About Sharks and How To Save Them* (National Geographic Kids, 2016). Ruth is also a naturalist and lucky hitchhiker on ocean research cruises including diving to the deep sea. Find out more at www.ruthamusgrave.com.

www.rourkeeducationalmedia.com

Special Thanks to ARCUS.ORG for their research and contributions.

PHOTO CREDITS: Cover foreground photo © gillmar—Shutterstock.com, cover bkground photo and title page ©R. Vickers—Shutterstock.com, card with paper clip art © beths—Shutterstock.com; contents page © SeventhDayPhotography I istockphoto.com; www.istock.com. www.shutterstock.com. PAGE 4-5: unUnlucky, TT, BlueDoorEd. PAGE 6-7: Elizabeth M. Ruggiero, Natalia Bratslavsky, ralphradford, DCrane08. PAGE 8-9: hlsnow, troutnut, mkrol.PAGE 10-11: National Park Service Photo, Bizi88, AdrianHancu. PAGE 12-13: R. Vickers, bl utack, USGS, USGS photo, Benjamin Jones. PAGE 14-15: Kjoland, Jonathan Mauer, coffeechcolate. PAGE 16-17: HaizhanZheng, aroderick, mlharing, NancyS, National Park Service Photo. PAGE 18-19: Melissa Barker (PolarTREC 2012), Courtesy of ARCUS, munro1, Ken Tape. PAGE 20-21: Lukas Bischoff, www.arcus.org, Amy Larsen-National Park Service, Sofiia Dorsey, Viktor Loki, www.arcus.org. PAGE 22-23: YGH, SeventhDayPhotography, Sergey Uryadnikov, John Pennell. PAGE 24-25: National Park Service Images. PAGE 26-27: National Park Service Images. PAGE 28-29: webguzs, oksanaphoto, redfishweb, Frank van Manen, USGS. PAGE 30-31: Master Sgt. Keith Brown-USMIL, Chase Dekker, Chilkoot. PAGE 32-33: CLP Media, mlharing, Bob Pool, Schaef1. PAGE 34-35: National Park Service/ Jeff Rasic, National Park Service. PAGE 36-37: National Park Service Images. PAGE 38-39: Drying Fish and caribou photos courtesy of NPS, E.F Leffingwell, National Park Service, Jakub Jerabek, Darryl Brooks. PAGE 40-41: Delpixart, page 40 inset photo © Paxson Woelberhttps://creativecommons.org/licenses/by-sa/3.0/deed.en. PAGE 42-43: NPS/Matt Cameron, Jiri Kulisek. PAGE 44-45: National Park Service, Molly E Tedesche.

Edited by: Keli Sipperley

Produced by Blue Door Education for Rourke Educational Media. Cover design by: Nicola Stratford; Interior design and layout by: Jennifer Dydyk

Gates of the Arctic / Ruth A. Musgrave
  (Natural Laboratories: Scientists in National Parks)
  ISBN 978-1-64369-024-7 (hard cover)
  ISBN 978-1-64369-115-2 (soft cover)
  ISBN 978-1-64369-171-8 (e-Book)
Library of Congress Control Number: 2018956029

Printed in the United States of America, North Mankato, Minnesota